MW01658234

PRAISE FOR R.J. FOX

With a gut-busting blend of dry wit and delicious self-deprecation, R.J. Fox is the new spokesperson for those of us who bumped and bruised a path through adolescence.

—Frank Morelli, author of *No Sad Songs*

Growing up can be tough, and R.J. doesn't hold back in delivering the explosive melancholia of dealing with it, while keeping the tone sweet.

—Vincent Daniels,
author of *Meaty Balls* and *Holly Jolly Nothing*

Fox's collection reminds us of a simpler time of being simply miserable, but does so with true heart and humor. His knack for telling painful stories in an honest, hilarious fashion makes him a necessary storyteller in these divisive times.

—Michael A. Ferro, author of *TITLE 13: A Novel*

R.J. has created a funny and well-written collection, but at the same time a slightly painful and sadly accurate depiction of life back when bullying was just "kids being kids."

—Randy D Pearson,
author of *Driving Crazy* and *Trac Brothers*

With his droll sense of humor, R.J. Fox joins the ranks of writers like David Sedaris, Spalding Gray, Garrison Keillor, and Jean Shepherd.

—Anne Gauteau

Left me reeling in wonder as to the depths of human cruelty yet charmed by the fortitude of one's resilience.

—Melissa Grunow, author of *Realizing River City*

R.J. Fox shares the honest struggles of growing up highlighting the often-tough social situations with our peers that rocked our core. Reading this work pushes us to consider how the roles that others have played in our lives shape who we are today. And likewise, the impact we have had on others.

—Lori Roddy,
Executive Director of the Neutral Zone

TALES FROM THE DORK SIDE

R.J. FOX

FIFTH AVENUE PRESS

CONTENTS

TALES FROM THE DORK SIDE

R. J. Fox

Tales from the Dork Side

Editor: Alex Kourvo / Cover: Phil McMullen

Fifth Avenue Press is a locally focused and publicly owned publishing imprint of the Ann Arbor District Library. It is dedicated to supporting the local writing community by promoting the production of original fiction, non-fiction and poetry written for children, teens and adults.

Printed in the United States of America

First Printing, 2017

ISBN: 978-1-947989-06-1 (Paperback); 978-1-947989-07-8 (e-book)

Fifth Avenue Press

305 S Fifth Ave

Ann Arbor, MI 48104

fifthavenue.press

for Lillian and Bobby.
Never give up.

1

TIPS FOR AVOIDING THE DORK SIDE

If you don't want to be a dork, don't spend spring break of your senior year riding a carousel.

- Avoid bragging about your Magic Rocks, no matter how large or how colorful.

- Never admit that you prefer playing with My Little Pony and Barbie dolls over He-Man and G.I. Joe.

- Don't wear your plastic Sea-Monkey necklace to school.

- If you are perpetually teased and bullied by your classmates, avoid being friends with someone who tells people he lays eggs.

- Avoid leaving a pair of dirty underpants in the pant leg of your jeans. Otherwise, it might work its way out throughout the course of the day, revealing itself to everyone as you come out of a bathroom with it trailing behind you in all of its white, poop-streaked glory, as one of your tormentors proclaims, "Look! His underwear is hanging out of his pants! And there's streaks!" Moreover, don't try to hide said underwear by picking it up and shoving it back down your pants.

- Don't stick your arm between two booths at Dairy Queen, unless you want to get it stuck, requiring someone to dismantle an entire booth in order to rescue your arm. Especially don't do this if a girl you have a crush on is sitting nearby, eating ice cream with her family.

- Spending summer days cooped up in your basement watching your Lionel train go around in circles while listening to Weird Al Yankovic won't improve your social life.

- When going down a waterslide, it's always a good idea to make sure your bathing suit is fastened properly, lest it fall off and land twenty feet away from where you are left standing, fully nude.

- Don't wear a fanny pack. If you do, don't refer to your fanny pack as your jet propulsion device. And even if you aren't teased and bullied by your classmates, don't wear a fanny pack.

- Don't boast about going to a New Kids on the Block concert. Bragging that you saw it in a suite will only make it worse.

- Make sure your mother doesn't glue fake eyebrows made out of cotton balls to your real eyebrows when you are supposed to dress up as an old man for a school assembly. Otherwise, upon removal of the fake eyebrows, one—and only one—of your real eyebrows might literally come off. You will then be called Bobby Eyebrow for the rest of the school year.

- Don't let your classmates see a picture of you dressed up as a cheerleader.

- Don't tell your classmates that your mom works for Lifeline (from the infamous "I've fallen and I can't get up!" commercials), even if she works at a hospital and is responsible for answering Lifeline calls. They will never, ever let it go.

- If you're still using training wheels in fourth grade, it's best not to let your friends see you on your bike. Ever.

- It's probably a good idea to end your belief in Santa Claus and the Easter Bunny before you reach the sixth grade.

- Don't assume that becoming a Bugle Boy model is going to help you gain popularity. Having a wardrobe of one hundred percent Bugle Boy clothes will only lead to being called Bugle Dork.

- If you have a crush on one of the most popular girls in the school, avoid writing her a note with the question, "Will you go out with me?" followed by two check boxes marked *yes* and *no*. She will share said note with all her friends before replying back with a resounding "No!" as she hands your note to you. And the *no* box will not only be checked off, but highlighted. Being a Bugle Boy model will not help you.

- Don't tell your crush that the reason you are sticking the rotating Slimer at the top of your Ghostbusters-themed pen up your nose is because it is a breathing device.

- Attempting to style your hair like Vanilla Ice or Zack Morris will do nothing to boost your social standing.

- Don't let on to your middle school peers that you are scared that fireworks will put a hole in the sky or that *Sesame Street* characters live inside the air vents of your car.

- Avoid, at all costs, the temptation to pee your pants while playing in the snow at recess. Especially early recess, when you have to spend the remainder of the day with your pants full of piss. Telling your classmates that you smell funny because of your mom's new laundry detergent will not fool anyone.

- If you attempt to fight back against one of your bullies, make sure you make it a direct hit, not a half-assed slap that just barely grazes his cheek. A tiny slap will only lead to more teasing from both your bully and all the witnesses.

- Digging holes in the dirt beneath the swing set while the rest of your peers are playing sports won't help you gain popularity. If other classmates join in, don't refer to yourself as "First Boss" in an effort to establish your turf. You will never be first boss.

2

LEAD OFF

Modeling my prized Casio Watch while drinking a two liter of Faygo Redpop.

I AM NOT AN ATHLETE. Never was and never will be.

And yet, I love sports.

It's an unfortunate mismatch. Just like growing up in the great sports town of Detroit with a dad who never watched them. How is a boy supposed to learn?

I was always short for my age. I was the last in my class to reach puberty. I never stood a chance. If it weren't for participation trophies, I wouldn't have a single one.

Like most kids, my sports training began in elementary school gym class. It didn't take long for me—or anyone else for that matter—to realize that I wasn't a natural born athlete, nor was I one in training. And losing doesn't always have to do with keeping score. It's one thing to suck at sports. It's a whole other kind of suck to get laughed at for sucking at sports. That was my elementary school and middle school in a nutshell. Even my gym teacher made fun of me.

So why was I so bad at physical education? Of course, being small for my age had a lot to do with it, but one of the most athletic boys in my class was actually shorter than me. He was also my biggest bully. The crux of the problem is, I never really know what direction I'm heading. As long as I'm going straight, my mind automatically thinks it's heading north. It's hard to play sports if you have no spatial reasoning.

At least during team sports like dodgeball, I could sort of slip between the cracks and hide out of view, flinching before the ball was even thrown. With solo acts like chin-ups and rope climbing, there was nowhere to hide. A spotlight shone on my shame as my legs dangled helplessly beneath me.

Then there was soccer. The true highlight of my illustrious soccer career was being known as the weird little boy who stood in the middle of the field during the game, staring incessantly at his digital, waterproof Casio watch, counting down the minutes until the game was over so he could be put out of his misery.

This watch-staring habit got so out of hand at school that my teacher had to bring my parents in for a talk. Their solution? Take my watch away during games. Now, instead of being the weirdo who stood in the middle of the soccer field constantly staring at my watch, I was the weirdo who stood in the middle of the field staring at the skin on my wrist where the watch used to be.

I lasted one season.

In T-ball, I hit the tee more than the ball. In gymnastics, I merely flailed around. Maybe organized sports weren't for me. I needed something I could do at my own pace.

It was around this time that I decided to branch out and try my hand at skateboarding, which was almost impossible to avoid as an 80s child. Sensing an opportunity to improve my social standing, I begged my parents for a skateboard of my own. I should have had the foresight to realize that my lack of coordination was probably not a good fit for skateboarding, but I was willing to look beyond that if it meant any chance to be seen as cool. Of course, it was important to get a legitimate, authentic wooden skateboard like all the cool kids and pros used. Instead, my parents bought me a cheap, blue plastic skateboard that was about half the width of a standard skateboard. It might as well have been Fisher-Price. Not only was I teased for it, but I never quite got the hang of the whole balancing component required to navigate a skateboard, wiping out endlessly to the tune of several minor, but irritating scrapes and bruises.

After a few weeks, I used my skateboard for the sole purpose of rolling down the driveway in the sitting position.

Onward to middle school, the nadir of my bullied youth. If I could sum up my middle school experience in one singular moment, it would be getting plunked in the noggin by a basketball heaved over the gymnasium balcony, resulting in a direct hit to my skull. The bounce was breathtaking. And the impact not only knocked me off my feet, but I saw stars. Honest-to-goodness *stars.*

After two hellish years, it was time to start at Edsel Ford High School, whether I was ready or not. The combination of my short and scrawny stature and being in the marching band was not exactly a winning combination for an incoming high school freshman.

I will never forget the first day of band camp, already feeling nervously out of place and overhearing an upperclassman proclaim, "Look how little he is!"

I wasn't even safe from getting picked on in *marching band.*

Things really began to look up in the summer of tenth grade when I magically grew several inches and *finally* hit puberty. However, despite being taller, my athletic skill did not grow along with me. In gym class, I consistently finished second to last in the two-mile run. The kid who finished last was closing in on 300 pounds.

During my pivotal sophomore year, I asked for a weight set for Christmas. Technically, they were very strong rubber bands, but still a major "upgrade" from the five-pound dumbbells I had received for my birthday in sixth grade. It was time to put some meat on my bones. That same Christmas, I also received Michael Jackson's *Dangerous* CD, which I exercised to vigorously. I can't say I got any stronger, or more dangerous, but I certainly felt so mentally.

After a few months, most of the rubber bands had either snapped, or were on the verge of snapping. Putting safety first, I quit. I wouldn't lift weights again for ten years.

And despite my full awareness of how awful I was at sports, it wasn't enough to stop me from trying. During my junior year, I tried out for both baseball and basketball. I was not only cut in the first round in both sports, I was the first one cut, period.

Over the years, I have continued to try my hand at a variety of other athletic endeavors. Every now and then, when the planets are aligned with Pluto, I'm prone to brief flashes of athletic competence, but it never takes me long to come back to Earth.

Despite my failings, nothing has stopped me from attempting curling, ice-skating, bowling, bocce ball, putt-putt, bean-bag toss, lawn darts, horseshoes, badminton, Frisbee, volleyball and, last, but not least, Wallyball, which aesthetically resembles the white-padded cell of an insane asylum. However, in Wallyball, the walls don't have pads. They are made of concrete. And they hurt. As for the game itself, Wallyball is volleyball inside a racquetball court—the bumper bowling of volleyball. But years of losing taught me an important lesson.

The only true way to lose was to give up.

And not giving up was the one thing I have consistently won at.

My moment of glory was just around the corner. There was one brief, shining day when I started to win.

But it took me a lifetime of losing to get there.

3

TREE HUGGER

That isn't a Michael Jackson cassette tape I'm listening to. It's Weird Al Yankovic.

SOME KIDS SPEND warm afternoons in the safe confines of a tree house. For one afternoon, at the tender age of nine, I had the luxury of spending mine tied to a tree.

Following a half-day of school, I was walking home, eagerly anticipating my mom's yummy egg salad when I approached Teddy Thompson's house. Teddy Thompson was one of the few jocks who—on most days—was actually nice to me. Every now and then, he would invite me over to play. However, the moment someone else spotted us together, he conveniently turned against me. So our friendship was, for lack of a better description, closeted.

When I passed by his house, he stepped out onto the porch and eagerly invited me in. This presented an instant dilemma. Should I delay egg salad sandwich gratification in exchange for a rare opportunity for social interaction? Or stick to my game plan? I decided egg salad could wait. Who knew when I would next be invited to someone's house to play?

Especially a cool person.

When I arrived at Teddy's house, three other classmates were already there. And two of those three classmates were among my biggest tormenters: Matt Belcher and David Murphy. And with no sign of parental supervision, the odds were not on my side. But there was no turning back. If I walked out the door, I would probably be subject to more ridicule than if I stayed. Then again, most of it would be behind my back, so maybe that wouldn't have been such a bad thing. I ultimately decided to stay put and prove I could hang with the in-crowd. Besides, they had pizza.

But first things first. I had to call home and ask for permission.

"May I use your phone?" I asked Teddy.

"Sure."

"Why, so you can call your mommy?" taunted Belcher.

"Yes. I need to call my mom."

Teddy showed me to the kitchen phone. As I dialed, I overheard their conversation.

"Why did you invite him over?" said Murphy.

"He's not that bad," said Teddy.

"He's a dork. And the biggest mama's boy," said Murphy, really fixated on this whole mommy thing. Who did he think I was, Norman Bates?

"Don't worry. I got a plan…" I heard Teddy say, before my mom finally picked up.

"Hi. Can I play at Teddy Thompson's?"

"Teddy Thompson? Sure!" my mom said, probably trying to hide her excitement about the fact that her son was actually invited to someone's house.

"Okay, thanks. Love you."

"I love you, too."

Laughter poured out of the other room as I hung up. When I entered the room, I was greeted with a taunting echo of my own voice. "I love you, Mommy."

"Guys, stop," Teddy pleaded.

"Is there any pizza left?" I asked.

"Nope!" boasted Belcher, shoving the last piece into his mouth, proceeding to live up to his name by letting out a loud belch.

I pretended not to let it bother me, despite being so darn hungry. There would always be egg salad.

We headed out into the backyard to play wiffle ball, or so I was lead to believe. I knew something was amiss when I noticed the rope. My next clue was when my tormentors began to push me toward the giant oak tree looming in the center of the yard.

I did not resist. I knew better.

Teddy stood by, doing nothing to stop it. Clearly, this was the "plan" he was referring to.

Did he lure me to his house with this plan in mind all along?

Or was he simply caving into peer pressure? I would have plenty of time to ask myself these questions later. Belcher and Murphy held me in place with my back against the trunk as Teddy grabbed the rope and proceeded to wrap it around my body.

"If you scream, we will kill you," Belcher threatened.

Meanwhile, Teddy tightened the rope around my ankles. When they were done, Murphy reiterated Belcher's earlier claim. "If you tell anyone," Murphy stared me in the eye, "we will hunt you down. And kill you."

I never told anyone until years later when it was too late to file charges.

Teddy and his merry band of tormentors began to dance around the tree, patting their hands on their mouths in a grotesque imitation of Native Americans.

As I struggled to free myself, the rope began to loosen, but Murphy noticed and this time, tied the rope so tight it dug into my stomach.

But then salvation came in the form of an elderly neighborhood grouch.

"Stop hitting your damn balls into my yard!"

The neighbor proceeded to toss a wiffle ball back over the fence. She either didn't notice that a boy was tied to a tree, or assumed that boys were just being boys. Or, simply didn't give a shit. All that mattered was that I'd lost a perfect shot at liberation.

My captors proceeded to play ball as I helplessly watched from my vantage point in centerfield. A steady barrage of wiffle balls were aimed in my general direction. And my limbs were helpless to deflect them.

Fortunately, only two or three actually hit me. One was a welt-producing shot to the center of my forehead. It took every ounce of strength not to scream for mercy, fearful of retribution.

When they had their fill of playing ball, Murphy approached me and put a bunch of dry leaves under my feet. Belcher removed a pack of matches from his pocket and attempted to set the leaves on fire, which I managed to stomp out. In retaliation, Murphy attempted to set the rope on fire, but I blew out the match.

Twice.

The third time, Belcher put his hand over my mouth to allow Murphy to complete his task. Fortunately, the rope wouldn't ignite and even more fortunately, lighter fluid never crossed his mind. After several attempts, he gave up, with a half-hearted plea from Teddy to "cut it out." Belcher and Murphy listened, which prompted Teddy to suggest that they head off to a park "to hit some real baseballs." I wasn't included in this plan. The plan for me was to stay tied to the tree, which was certainly better than being set on fire.

A silver lining, as it were.

Left behind, all I could think about was freedom. And egg salad sandwiches. But would I ever see home again? Would I be left here for dead? Would crows peck out my eyeballs? Is this how Jesus felt? What would Jesus do?

To this day, I'm claustrophobic and hate being confined. There is no doubt in my mind that this is where it started.

All I needed was for somebody to pass by and freedom would be mine.

But the only thing that passed by was time.

The bells of a neighborhood church let me keep track of time in 15 minute increments. After an hour, the afternoon sun began to beat down on my face, which caused me to sweat, attracting mosquitoes to my face like moths to light.

And unbeknownst to me, my greatest humiliation was literally just around the corner.

It started out promising enough. Approaching voices. I

could taste freedom on my lips. And freedom tasted like egg salad sandwiches.

But freedom has a price. And that price was in the form of the three most popular girls from my class, including Nicki Smith, my biggest crush. Why couldn't it have been an adult neighbor walking a dog?

As much as I yearned for freedom, I prayed Nicki wouldn't see me. I would rather spend the night tied to that tree than be seen there by the girl of my dreams. I knew full well that any chance I had with her would be obliterated if she saw me like this. Then again, perhaps she would have felt so bad for me, she would have fell for me on sympathy alone.

Who was I kidding? I wanted to disappear.

If there was one thing I had learned by the tender age of nine, it was that fate could be cruel. And that this was just one of many embarrassments I would endure throughout my lifetime regarding the opposite sex.

As the girls drew nearer, I held my breath. At first, nobody seemed to notice, but as soon as one of the girls pointed a finger, I knew it was over.

"Look!" one of Nicki's friends said, laughing hysterically.

I bowed my head—the only thing I could do to conceal my identity, even though it was probably already too late. Maybe if I played it cool, they would just assume I *wanted* to be affixed to the tree.

They continued to laugh *and* they continued walking, leaving me hanging, even though for one fleeting moment, I am almost certain I saw pity on Nicki's face. In all likelihood, it was probably a hallucination caused by the sweltering heat and vision obscured by mosquitoes, which were now nesting in my eyebrows.

Despite a missed opportunity for rescue, I tried not to panic. After all, it could have been worse, like that scene in *Titanic* when they see a ship out in the distance, which doesn't see them in return. Eventually, either my mother would come looking for me, or Teddy's parents would come home. Right? My captors would probably set me free before it got to that point to avoid getting in trouble.

The church bells chimed two. Then three. Sometime between three and four, my captors returned. Teddy approached me with a knife. His friends trailed behind. My initial thought was that I was about to be gutted like a fish. But instead, Teddy took the knife and cut the rope, despite pleas from his friends to leave me there even longer.

I was a free man.

"If you tell anybody about this, next time, we will kill you," Belcher warned one last time. I took heed. Part of me still fears that writing this will somehow lead to retaliation.

I ran home as fast as I could, just in case my tormentors changed their mind. My mother greeted me at the door and suddenly, all was right with the world. I promptly fed my pet Sea-Monkeys, comforted by the thought that—unlike my classmates—they would never let me down.

"Did you have fun?" my mother asked.

I considered telling her the truth, but chose life instead.

"Yeah. Lots," I said, making every effort to sound convincing.

"So what did you do?" my mother asked, probably relieved that her son was actually invited over to someone's house to play.

"Played wiffle ball."

"Did you eat?"

"There was pizza."

"Are you hungry?"

"Yeah, a little."

I was *starving*.

She promptly removed the egg salad out of the fridge, which almost made everything I had endured worth it.

Even now, I wonder if Teddy Thompson ever regretted his role in what transpired that day. Maybe someday, I'll ask him. But deep down, I already know the answer. Bullies don't regret what they do. Most of the time, they don't even remember.

But I'll never forget.

4

WELT

If you're trying to rise on the social ladder, you'll need a better Halloween costume than bad face paint and cardboard ears.

GETTING PICKED last in gym class is a death sentence to the social life of a boy. But really, I was hopeless in gym class even when we weren't picking teams. Chin-ups and rope climbing were one and the same to me, as they achieved the same effect —failure and shame.

When forced to attempt chin-ups, my skinny legs dangled helplessly beneath me as I strained to elevate my chin above the bar. One would think being a frail, skinny child would have made this feat easier. It did not. As I hung from the bar like a sheet hung out to dry on a calm day, I saw all my classmates watching down below.

Laughing.

Climbing a rope was a similar ordeal, but rather than my legs dangling in the air, they would straddle the rope like a dog humping a flopping fish. I always ended up exactly where I started, at the bottom of the rope, but with newly chafed hands.

I would suffer a similar humiliation in middle school when I attended an adventure camp that required me to climb an enormous, outdoor climbing wall. I got no farther than ten feet up before losing my grip and crashing back into the wall as I hung from my harness. Meanwhile, the rest of my classmates made it all the way up with seemingly little to no effort.

My fear of heights, combined with my lack of physical coordination was the driving force behind my decision to pass on an adventure ropes course suspended high above the treetops. I didn't even deliberate on this one. Of course, my refusal to do it only lead to more humiliation from my peers than had I at least attempted it.

I fared no better at recess. Unlike most kids, I dreaded recess. I preferred the relatively safe, supervised confines of a classroom. More specifically, I dreaded the ample opportunity it brought for my bullies to find fresh and exciting ways to torment me. While the cool kids played sports during recess, I dug holes in the dirt beneath the swing set, far away from the athletic field where my classmates played and increased their ever-growing popularity.

As though gym and recess weren't humiliating enough, my last name in itself brought a whole other degree of ridicule. And it was all due to the popular childhood game, "What Time is it, Mr. Fox?"

My experience with this game often went something like this:

"What time is it, Mr. Fox?"

"Time to kick your butt!"

Which, by the time I reached middle school, morphed into, "Time to kick your ass!"

However, none of these challenges measured up to my true elementary school nemesis, dodgeball—the bane of every elementary school dork, freak, and other form of social outcast. There's something inherently flawed about a game where the object is to throw something at somebody. Not *to* them, so they can catch it, but *at* them, so you can hit them as hard as possible. In some ways, dodgeball is a tamer version of boxing. Of course, no school would ever dare force students to box, but dodgeball is just dandy.

Some might even argue that football is more brutal than dodgeball. That might be true, but when football is played in gym class, tackling is prohibited. Furthermore, the primary aim of football is not tackling, but rather to bring the ball over the goal line. In dodgeball, violence is the *only* goal. It's the elementary school rendition of survival of the fittest.

The original *Hunger Games.*

The sinister origins of dodgeball can be traced back over six hundred years. Originally played in Africa, there are early variations on record in Korea, China, and Germany. In the game's earliest incarnation, the game wasn't played with rubber balls. It was played with rocks. In that context, I guess I should count my blessings.

In the early days, once an individual was struck, their opponents continued to pelt them until they were finished off for good. It was up to the struck man's teammates to defend their fallen comrade by pelting the attackers with rocks of their own. This ritual was believed to encourage tribal teamwork in preparation for skirmishes against other tribes. It also helped weed out the weak.

With the exception of rocks, not much has really changed.

In the late 1800s, an English missionary named Dr. James H. Carlisle witnessed the ruthless game, and introduced a "tamer" version of the game back home. In place of rocks was a leather ball, which was still painful, only less lethal. In this more domesticated version, smacking somebody with a ball simply wasn't enough. A player was only knocked out of the game if they were knocked to the ground. If they remained standing after a blow, they remained in the game.

A few years later, the game made its way over to the U.S. with the first official rules drawn up in 1905. Soon, colleges across the country were playing one another in competition, opening the floodgates for school-sanctioned, team sport bullying. Instead of having to throw objects at victims when authority figures weren't looking—or, in some cases, *were* looking—bullies were now actually encouraged to take aim.

Anybody who has ever played the modern version of dodgeball understands there are a few types of participants. There are the *cowerers* and the *champions*. The gap between the eventual loser and eventual winner couldn't be any wider. The champions manage to knock off most of their opponents, while simultaneously avoiding getting hit themselves. The cowerers? Not so much. The *in-betweeners* are the middle ground between the champions and the cowerers. At least they tried. And then there are the *early birds*. These are the participants who are smart enough to pretend to get hit amidst the chaos of the game's opening shots, in an effort to avoid getting hit for real, sparing themselves the pain associated with actually getting nailed by a ball. Looking back, I should have settled for the early bird option. But I was always a cowerer.

Cowerers outlast almost everybody—not out of sheer athleticism, but for the sole reason that they spend the entire game glued to the back wall, cowering in fear, using everyone else as human shields. As the others are eliminated one by one, cowerers suddenly emerge as easy targets because there is nowhere else to hide. It is only a matter of time before cowerers meet their maker. Unlike the participants who got knocked out unnoticed amidst the early chaos of the game, the eyes of the entire class get to now witness your demise as you, the noble cowerer, run back and forth against the wall in this most dangerous game, until you find yourself curled defensively into a ball on the floor, awaiting your inescapable fate.

For me, games of dodgeball more often than not came down to myself and my nemesis, David Murphy.

Bully #1.

David, of course, was a natural at this game, licking his chops at any opportunity to play, even going so far as to beg the gym teacher to squeeze in a game at the end of class. For David, life was one huge, never-ending dodgeball game. Presumably, my gym teacher was no different than David Murphy when he was a kid. The only difference between the two was a teaching certificate.

If there was one silver lining, it was that the jocks were more concerned about knocking out other jocks in a demonstration of their uber-competitive jockiness. It wasn't that David was especially athletic. He wasn't. It came down to the fact that this game was a bully's paradise, allowing him to pluck out the weak one by one, usually followed by the more athletically inclined in the class, who could easily beat David in every other sport on the planet, except dodgeball.

David always left me for last. This allowed him to maximize the humiliation he relished. Like a predatory cat with an injured mouse, David taunted and tortured me by intentionally missing me six or seven times to prolong my misery. To the amusement of the entire class, I cowered in the fetal position, where I remained until the gym teacher finally, reluctantly, told him to finish. Then David would plunk me and have a celebratory dance like a cocky receiver after a touchdown, as if he'd done something difficult.

David even organized playground versions of the game, independent from gym class. It was the only organizing he was capable of, but boy did he put his all into that. David always sought me out on the playground to join in. Unlike gym class, where the game was mandated, I could have opted out of the playground version, focusing instead on digging to China beneath the swing set. But I was driven by fear, with no choice but to take my lumps.

Fortunately, after generations of traumatized youth, dodgeball has been banned by many schools across the nation. Where it isn't banned yet, rubber balls have been replaced with softer sponge balls, the kind that don't leave welts. I was not so lucky.

Twenty years later, an unexpected opportunity for redemption arrived in the form of a dodgeball tournament aboard a Royal Caribbean cruise. I was naturally hesitant at first. An entire childhood plagued with dodgeball and now I was expected to volunteer for it? For fun?

But what did I have left to lose? Even if I totally sucked, I could prove I was no longer afraid. And maybe, just maybe, I had a shot at success. Maybe, just maybe, I could purge my childhood demons once and for all.

Perhaps it had to do with the abundance of fruity cocktails

I'd consumed. Or perhaps it was the strong Caribbean breeze aboard our vessel, making it difficult for the lightweight ball to soar more than five feet, which somehow made everything seem less intimidating.

Suddenly, my first taste of athletic confidence took over my body.

The tournament began. My team was comprised of all age groups, spanning all walks of life. I sat on the sidelines, eagerly awaiting our chance to take the court.

When my team finally took the court, I took several shots, all of which missed their intended target. Eclipsing my confidence was a simmer of frustration. I wanted to do better. But as the game progressed, my teammates went down one by one. By some divine miracle, not only was I still standing, but I was no longer using my teammates as body shields. I'd suddenly become aggressive.

Driven, like an animal.

No longer a cowerer, I charged toward every ball, rather than dodging them.

I was silently disqualified in the middle of the pack, not by a bean, but by an opponent's legal catch. It was a worthy throw, caught by an even more worthy opponent—a college-aged fratboy. This was as close to redemption as I was going to get. And I could live with that. I could finally hang 'em with fearless grace. This was no *Rocky* moment, but I didn't need one. All I needed to know was that I could stand tall. I could throw the ball. I didn't have to be afraid.

I was no longer a cowerer.

5

THE DOGSHIT INCIDENT

The defining moment of my childhood took place on the snow-covered playground of my elementary school. I was in fourth grade. Most children can't wait until the recess bell rings, but for me, recess was a lonely, frightening place.

Like most days, I had spent half of recess digging a hole in the dirt with my fellow dork friend Patrick, while all the other boys played football in the snow. Tired of digging, I headed over to the slide.

As I prepared to go down for the eighth time—this time, on my stomach—I spotted my number one tormentor heading my way: David Murphy.

This dipshit gave me trouble from the moment he arrived in the second grade, which at least spared me two years of torture. My first encounter with David was in the bathroom, where he pulled out what looked like an old school switchblade on me while I was taking a whiz with my brown-bagged lunch nestled under my arm (lovingly labeled "Bobby" with a heart around it). David snatched it from me. As I attempted to shield my face from a potential knife attack, I dribbled piss all down the front of my pants, which I suppose was better than getting slashed by a knife.

"Need a diaper, little boy?" David laughed like a maniac before he revealed to me that his "blade" was actually a plastic comb. Yeah, the joke was on me. He laughed all the way out of the bathroom and down the hall like a villain from a cheesy teen comedy.

Two years later, I still hadn't learned how to defend myself against David Murphy and his friends. They were multiplying with each passing year

There seemed to be no method to David's madness. Sometimes, days or even weeks passed before I fell victim to his antics. There were stretches where he struck multiple times a day. Like every great terrorist, he thrived on the element of surprise.

As I sat on top of the slide, David watched from below with a sinister grin. I felt like a cat chased up a tree by a rabid mutt. There was no way this could end well. I waited several minutes then realized that I could possibly escape trouble by backing down the ladder, undetected. But it made no difference, other than to maybe delay my undeserved comeuppance.

I glanced over at Patrick, who was still digging away in the dirt, oblivious to everything. Not that he could have done anything to help. In fact, he was probably the next victim.

I took a deep breath and slid down, expecting the worst. David greeted me at the bottom and grabbed me by the scruff of the neck like a helpless kitten. Per usual, my teacher was nowhere in sight. Why was this always the case?

"What's up, dork?" David asked.

I didn't respond. But he demanded an answer.

"I said, *what's up dork?*"

"Nothing," was the best I could offer.

"Come with me," he demanded.

Patrick finally looked up from his digging, but we both knew there was nothing he could do. I didn't take it personally. We both knew it wouldn't be any different when our roles were inevitably reversed. It was only natural that any friend of mine would be a target for David Murphy. What we both needed were friends who had each other's backs, rather than the kind who scampered off at any sign of trouble. But once branded a dork, there was really no turning back.

"Get down on your knees, dork!" David commanded.

As always, I did as he asked of me. But then I saw it.

A frozen pile of dogshit.

"Lick it," David insisted.

"Please, no," I begged.

"Lick it, before I make you eat it."

I froze in terror.

"Lick it or eat it, dork!"

By now, a small group of classmates, including my number one crush—Nicki Smith—stood around to watch with morbid curiosity. Some were probably relieved that they were being spared for the time being. Though most weren't exactly cheering David, nobody was going out of their way to stop him, either.

Nicki's expression suggested some degree of concern, which gave me hope, though she did nothing to help. Nobody did. Patrick, meanwhile, continued to dig a hole, perhaps plotting his escape.

And again, where in the hell was my goddamn teacher? My only saving grace was for my teacher to witness one of my daily tortures, so she could see for herself. Once would be all it would take. Or, would it even make a difference? But I wasn't going to be able to see for myself that day. And I wasn't going to bank on the next day, either. It was up to me—and only me—to defend my honor.

"Do it!" David shouted, pointing to the frozen turd pile.

Like the shit itself, I was also frozen, using all my strength to resist. This was the closest I had ever come to resisting a bully. The line was drawn. All it took was a frozen pile of dogshit.

David placed his hand on my neck and whispered, "If you don't lick this shit, I'm going to force feed it to you. Do I make myself clear, *dork?* Last chance!"

But like a determined fighter, I refused to go down for the count. I held my ground. No matter how much I continued to resist, David continued to physically lower my face toward my brown, frozen fate. At this point, I lost all sense of my surroundings. The world could have ended for all I knew. Nothing else existed. Just me, David Murphy, and a turd.

Inch, by inch, centimeter, by centimeter, David lowered my face toward the turdsicle. Textures and colors of the like I've never seen before began to reveal themselves to me. A layer of frozen crystals coated its entire surface, sparkling in the sunlight, only to lose their vibrant luster when the shadow of my face extinguished them. Or, was it the warmth of my face that melted them from their glowing existence?

As my face was pushed lower and lower toward its frozen brown bull's-eye, I resisted with all my might, but David continued pushing my face toward impending doggie-doo-doom, taking delight in the dramatic tension that was slowly developing.

"Open your mouth, dork!" David insisted, as he applied more pressure to my neck. Once again, I refused. David Murphy could take away my soul, but no matter how hard he tried, he couldn't make me open my mouth. I would die on this hill.

David continued to push on my neck. Hard. Before I knew it, the Hershey's kiss of death was grazing the tip of my nose, my cheeks, my forehead and ultimately, my lips. But I continued to resist, finding the strength to not get any closer to the discarded brownie. Sure, the texture scratched the surface of my flesh a little, but all things considered, I was quite lucky. It's a good thing it wasn't summer. I only had my face scratched by poo, not smeared by it.

And I never opened my mouth.

It was my victory.

When David decided that I'd had enough, he released my neck and uttered a dire warning. "If you tell anybody—"

"I won't," I said, thus sealing my fate. David now knew he could do it again.

Satisfied with my response, David ran off to join his friends in a friendly game of tetherball, where he proceeded to whack the ball with such force, it ended up smacking his friend's face.

Meanwhile, I returned to my favorite slide, filled with a sense of pride that I had survived yet another David Murphy attack.

Over the years, some have asked how I was able to cope with the David Murphys of the world. The answer is simple. I knew even then—yes, even while my face was shoved in dogshit—that I was going to be okay. That this was all a phase, rather than a lifetime sentence. Eventually, the David Murphys of the world would fade into oblivion as I passed by, bursting forth like a phoenix rising out of the ashes…or more specifically, a frozen pile of dogshit.

Not only did I know that I was going to be okay, but more importantly, I knew that David Murphy probably wouldn't be. Though I don't know whatever became of him, it wouldn't have come as a surprise to hear that he went to jail for stabbing somebody in a bar fight. Whether the victim would have deserved it or not, I have no clue. But in my experience, his victims rarely deserved it.

When it was all said and done, David Murphy was the biggest shit on the playground. And probably still is.

6

PECKING ORDER

My one moment of "cool."

I was labeled a nerd and a dork long before I learned to embrace these labels with pride. Back then, pride wasn't even in my vocabulary. When you are small for your age *and* chosen last in gym class, there really isn't much hope.

Socially, the pickings are slim. Fortunately, there were always other misfits to keep me company. However, not all dorks were my friends. There is an unwritten code in the dork kingdom that association with one another doesn't do a single thing to help the other's cause. We often avoid one another for the same reason the jocks avoided us.

When you're on the bottom of the social ladder, you compensate by shunning your own people, while simultaneously feeling yourself gravitating toward them as the only possible source of friendship, while the cool kids either reject you or fail to even notice that you exist.

It was simultaneously hypocritical and a defense mechanism.

A perpetual catch-22.

As a result, I had to endure other dorks who went out of their way to make fun of me just as much as the jocks did, because they were working so hard at being accepted. And so goes the world. A vicious circle.

To compound matters, I had friends over the years who chose to remain closeted when it came to being seen with me, for fear of being taunted themselves. Some of these individuals were fellow dorks. Some were several notches above me in the social pecking order, in borderline cool territory. They would invite me over to play when nobody else was around, but would then ignore me on the playground. Or, if they were playing with me on the playground, the moment another one of their friends showed up, they began taunting me. But I dealt with it because even a part-time friend was better than no friend at all.

Kids used one another mercilessly. For example, I had a Nintendo, but they didn't. Suddenly, my house was *the* house to hang out in. But when the Nintendo wasn't on, they wanted nothing to do with me. I was a single-purpose buddy.

One might ask how I could be so naïve. It wasn't so much naivety as being star struck by peers that under most circumstances either ignored me or bullied me. Even if I knew it was short-lived, it was still better than nothing. And maybe, just maybe, once they got to know me, they would want to be my friend 24/7, rather than just out of convenience. All it would take was one cool kid to treat me as one of them and perhaps all the rest would fall in line.

So maybe I *was* naïve.

Back in elementary school, amidst all the bullying I endured, I indulged in a lot of magical thinking. I managed to convince myself that all of my classmates were in on one big joke. One day, I would come to school and they would all yell "surprise!" and suddenly become my friends.

It never happened.

Then again, there was always Dan Wolocko. Dan Wolocko was one of the coolest kids in the class. And one of the most athletic. What separated him from his peers was the fact that he was perhaps the most genuinely nice guy in the entire school. He didn't have a mean bone in his body. And even though he was incapable of bullying me, he could have just ignored me like so many others. However, Dan always went out of his way to include me in playground activities. In gym class, when he was captain, he would sometimes pick me next-to-last, rather than dead last. More importantly, he often stood up for me in front of his buddies when he saw that they were harassing me. All it took was a simple "Guys, c'mon!" and they would step in line and leave me alone. At least, until the next day.

And although I never attended any of his birthday parties and wasn't even invited over one time, I still can't ever thank him enough for having my back at school.

As far as those beneath me in the social pecking order, I sometimes avoided them, too. I'm not proud of that, but it was my survival at stake. And I never stooped low enough to taunt them, no matter how desperate I was for acceptance by the popular crowd.

Which meant that I was often friendless. In the warped sense of social status that middle school affords a mid-level dork like myself, I was nestled squarely in a thorny no man's land.

I'm one hundred percent sure this is why I'm a writer now. After all, there is nothing a writer craves more than *attention.* Writing was a way to subconsciously defeat my bullies and come out on top, as well as a way for my introverted self to channel my extroverted self. I didn't have real friends, so I made some up. And really, my imaginary friends were much better than the bullies at school.

Over the years, I came to realize that those guys would *suck* as friends. Even so, in many ways, those bullies were the best thing that ever happened to me. I learned not to give a shit about what others thought of me. Now, I can look back at all of this stuff and laugh.

And then write about it.

7

SEA MONKEY NECKLACE

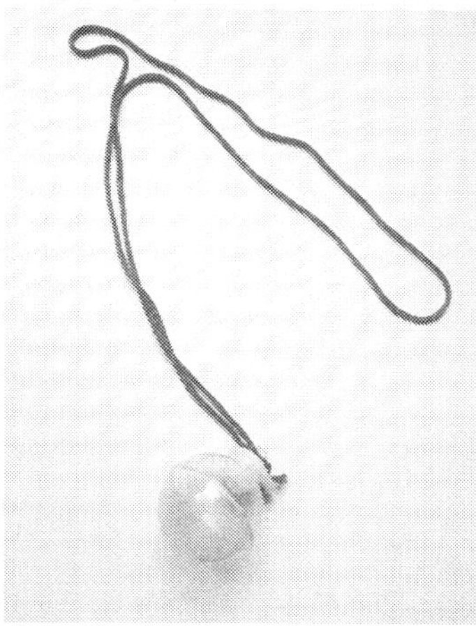

Yes, I still have it.

When you are a once-bullied child, you often think about going back in time and fixing your childhood. You think about it a lot. Sometimes you dream of changing the other kids, or changing the situation. Often, you think about changing yourself.

If I could talk to my childhood self, the first piece of advice I would give him is this: don't start out your fourth grade year sporting a Sea-Monkey necklace.

If you aren't fortunate enough to be already familiar, Sea-Monkeys are a hybrid form of brine shrimp that hatch instantly after adding water and are most commonly found in the science section at Toys "R" Us, next to Magic Rocks and ant farms. And unlike Uncle Milton's ants, Sea-Monkeys don't bite when given the opportunity.

Invented (or, more accurately marketed) in 1957 by Harold von Brauhut, Sea-Monkeys roughly resemble enlarged sperm, growing to a few inches in length. They look nothing like the picture on their package. They're advertised as long-limbed, mythical creatures with a dragon-like tail and three horns coming out of their heads. Sort of mermaid and magical. But never, at any point, would *monkey* be an accurate description.

According to their packaging, "Sea-Monkeys are a true miracle of nature. They exist in suspended animation inside their tiny eggs." That is, until water is added, making them "real life time travelers asleep in biological time capsules for their strange journey into the future!" The cherry on top is the fact that "anyone can get perfect results without any knowledge of chemistry or biology" which was ideal for a scientifically challenged youth like myself.

Like legions of other boys, I first discovered Sea-Monkeys advertised on the back of comic books. They were also sold in the Johnson-Smith Company catalog, which specialized in novelties like fake poop and snapping gum. How could I resist becoming the owner of "the most fantastic pets to ever live and breathe?" In fact, I was guaranteed to "have more fun with them than any aquatic creature you've ever owned. Unlike make-believe toys, pet Sea-Monkeys are really alive and are always ready and eager to put on a show!"

I got a deluxe Sea-Monkey kit for Christmas in first grade. It was love at first sight. And though my excitement for Sea-Monkeys has never worn off over the years, I will never forget my first time.

Fueling my excitement was the misguided assumption that they would look just like the package. They didn't. They looked like sperm cross-pollinated with a fetus. Despite my initial disappointment, I held steadfast to the belief that someday, they would live long enough to grow into the image of them depicted on the packaging. Part of me still believes.

Included in my starter kit was the traditional plastic aquarium. It also came with three small, color-coded, numbered packets. Packet #1: "Sea-Monkey Water Purifier." Packet #2: "Sea-Monkey Instant Life" (the eggs). Packet #3: "Sea-Monkey Growth Food." The kit included a double-sided spoon for feeding purposes: one side for baby Sea-Monkeys, the other for adults. The packet of food is so small, it raises the question: what happens when it runs out? However, I quickly learned that Sea-Monkeys usually don't outlive their food supply. And if by some rare miracle they do, replacement food can be ordered through the catalog.

One way to help make them live longer was to make use of the included "Sea-Monkey Million-Bubble Air Pump," which allows fresh oxygen to be manually pumped into the water. It can also be used to suck up feces, corpses of fallen Sea-Monkey comrades, and other debris.

Eager to hatch my new pets, I filled up the tank and added the water purifier, only to suffer through what every Sea-Monkey fan can relate to: the 24-hour waiting period before the eggs could be added. The wait to bring new life into the world was excruciating.

When the time finally came to add the "Instant Life"

packet, I spilled at least a quarter of the contents onto the counter. Once I rescued as many eggs as I could, I stirred the contents with a spoon for a full minute, setting forth in motion the miracle of life. After mixing my Sea-Monkey cocktail, I peered into the tank, but was unable to locate any discernible sign of life through the murky water. The legitimacy of the whole ordeal was brought into question. My dad promptly suggested that I hold the tank up to the window and into the light. Lo and behold, I noticed a hundred or so tiny, swimming specks, which were even more evident when seen through the numerous bubble magnifying glasses on the side of the tank.

After a few days, I no longer needed to find them through the magnifying glass.

Within a couple of weeks, Sea-Monkeys grow to about half an inch in size. Before long, up to three quarters of an inch, well on their way to becoming the humanesque caricatures on the package! Hope quickly faded into disappointment once I realized they weren't going to grow any larger, nor come close to the package's deceptive playful, carefree depiction in any size, shape, or form. In fairness, they did have long tails and horns on their heads, but it still begged the question: at what point does false advertising come into play?

Another disappointing early discovery was the alarming death rate. What started out as a bustling village of around a hundred living creatures was quickly cut in half. My initial thought was that they were sick. However, I would later come to realize that this was par for the course. Another week or so later, the Sea-Monkey apocalypse was reduced to a baker's dozen. The only upside to a smaller population was that I could give them names, such as Muffin, Cupcake, Cheesecake, Biff, Bert, Ernie, and Chet.

Sea-Monkeys, as one can imagine, are indeed, a most playful creature. The manual is chockfull of items that can be mail-ordered and sent directly to your doorstep! One of the items I ordered (for just one dollar, plus four dollars shipping and handling) were "Sea-Monkey Sea-Diamonds, the Anti-Gravity Toy." They came in a small packet similar to the Growth Food and Instant Life and contained small, plastic pebbles designed to look like diamonds. After dumping them into the water, they began to float at various levels of suspension. According to the product description, Sea-Monkeys were supposed to have a field day with them, tossing them back and forth like beach balls, playing soccer, or even surfing on them. In reality, the Sea-Monkeys ignored them, coming into contact with them only by accident. It sometimes even resulted in their death, if they were crushed beneath a lethal Sea-Diamond.

Other items I admit to ordering through the years: Grow-Kwickly Sea-Monkey Growth Stimulator, Red-Magic Sea-Monkey Vitamins, Sea-Medic Sea-Monkey Medicine, and Sea-Monkey Banana Treat. This last one was a banana-scented powder, because, what *monkeys* don't love bananas? There was even a mating powder (Cupid's Arrow) "for shy Sea-Monkeys afraid of marriage…this fabulous formula will give them a quick trip 'to the altar'! Once 'hooked,' former 'bachelor' Sea-Monkeys will fill your tank with oodles of babies—fast."

And finally, the best thing of all was the Sea-Monkey necklace. And by necklace, I don't mean a medallion resembling a Sea-Monkey. What I mean is, an actual miniature plastic bubble hanging from a red string that you can place a few of your Sea-Monkeys into (suctioned with the "Million Dollar Air Pump" of course!) and carry around town, or, in my case, school.

Despite constant teasing, I naturally convinced myself that they were jealous and/or didn't know a fashion statement when they saw one. Why the ladies didn't flock to me is something I'll never be able to figure out! Wearing it, I felt an overwhelming sense of protection, especially from bullies.

Never mind that the bullying was inspired to some degree by the necklace itself. It was a vicious cycle.

I will never forget that first day of school. I couldn't put that necklace on fast enough. But first, I had to carefully fill the bulb with my little buddies. Though I had my favorites, I took the first five sucked up by my pump. I felt bad for the ones who didn't make the pick, but there would be other days.

Or, so I thought.

My excitement that morning overshadowed the usual stomach ache I would get on the first day of school. In fact, I got stomach aches most days of school, elementary through middle school.

This year, I had an aquatic amulet to shield me, filled with an army of monkeys of the sea. Best of all, I would finally be able to share them with all my classmates, new and old alike. They had only *heard* about Sea-Monkeys at that point. I was certain that *this* would be the year I finally gained acceptance.

Well, I certainly got their attention. At first, nobody seemed to notice at all. But one by one, they all did. And though nobody was impressed, they were certainly entertained. Though some of my classmates were genuinely curious, I sure as hell wasn't going to start a Sea-Monkey craze. Perhaps if one of the cool kids did, it would have been a different story

"Hey, look! Bobby has a bowl of sperm around his neck!" one of my tormentors exclaimed.

My amulet was letting me down. And all its inhabitants could do was swim helplessly around. They had no clue. Ignorance truly was bliss.

And how in the hell did he even know what sperm was? Sex ed was still months away. Incidentally, the same kid who referred to my pets as sperm couldn't get his hands on my amulet quickly enough.

Fortunately, my teacher came to my aid, but only to scold

me. "Why don't I just hold on to these—whatever they are—for you. They are much too distracting."

So she put them in her desk, forcing my little buddies into darkness for the rest of the day.

I spent the rest of the day praying the necklace wouldn't leak.

When my teacher gave them back to me at the end of the day, she suggested that "Maybe they should stay at home where they belong."

Who was I to argue?

But that evening, I decided that I wasn't going to go down without a fight. From that point forward, I wore my amulet under my shirt. Its weight against my chest was oddly comforting and I was convinced I could hear soft, Sea-Monkey heartbeats in time with my own. Sometimes, it would leak, sending a warm trickle down my chest. Sometimes, the necklace gave off a nasty, musty odor, which, of course, did nothing to boost my social chances.

As far as Sea-Monkeys were concerned, my bullies loved to feign interest in my obsession and I was too gullible to even realize I was being teased. Or, maybe I was just in denial. I actually thought they'd be impressed by my lifetime membership in The Fellowship of the Secret Society of Sea-Monkey Scientists. Sometimes, I would share random facts. For example:

"Did you know, that NASA once flew Sea-Monkeys to outer space to test gravity's effect on animals born in a gravity-free environment? The result? They grew bigger and faster!"

"No! We didn't! Isn't that something, guys?" one of my bullies said, holding back laughter.

In the meantime, I cluelessly rambled on about the distinct personalities of my Sea-Monkeys, the way some kids would talk about their G.I. Joes, their pets, or their girlfriends. As an entire playground mocked me.

Looking back, it probably wasn't the wisest move to break down into tears as I described a Sea-Monkey spill and its subsequent rescue mission. Though most of my little buddies perished, I was able to single-handedly save three off the floor. Two others were squished.

But of all the random Sea-Monkey trivia I shared, the one thing that raised the most eyebrows was my insistence that Sea-Monkeys could rise from the dead. But I wasn't crazy. It's true! The trick is to let the water evaporate after every last Sea-Monkey is dead. Then add water. And *voila!* Instant life. *Hallelujah! Hallelujah!*

As though gym class wasn't bad enough, I decided to come to class one day wearing my amulet. I honestly assumed my teacher wouldn't give a shit.

"Fox!" my gym teacher shouted. "What are you doing with that damn thing on in gym class?"

For the record, this guy was as bad as my bullies. In fact, one couldn't create a more cliché gym teacher than this guy. If you were a jock, you were in his club. If not, you were a constant target, aided by his minions. Aka, my peers.

"Put it in your locker. Better yet, flush them down the damn toilet!"

This mandate was extended to the swimming pool, as well, simultaneously squashing my dream of swimming with my beloved pets and sparing them from death by chlorine.

My insistence on wearing the necklace raises a logical question. Well, probably several questions, but the main one is about my parents. Why didn't they try to stop me? Come to think of it, my parents certainly didn't help my cause on several occasions. But, looking back, I am eternally grateful that they didn't force me to leave my necklace at home, just as I'm grateful that—during that same year—they didn't talk me out of buying the Beastie Boys "License to Ill" album when they would have preferred that I buy the soundtrack to *Grease 2*, but I digress.

I still have Sea-Monkeys till this day. And I'm astounded by how little anything has changed. The packaging. The tank. The spoon. It's all timeless, suspended animation, much like Sea-Monkeys themselves.

Whenever I go into a toy store, I always make it a point to look for Sea-Monkeys and feel a tinge of disappointment when I don't see them. In fact, I gauge a toy store's worth by whether or not they carry Sea-Monkeys on their shelves. On a recent visit to Toys "R" Us, I noticed a variety of different types of tanks with various themes such as pirates, outer space, and even a pink tank aimed at girls, including a "Friendship Locket," the feminine equivalent of my necklace. If only I was able to find a female friend during childhood who shared my passion.

Not only do I still have Sea-Monkeys, but I still have my Sea-Monkey necklace, stored away in a box of childhood memories along with my fake poop and vomit. Every now and then, I consider filling the necklace up. Then I remember the teasing and leave it behind, but I will never leave behind the lessons it taught me.

8

MY AMERICAN PASTIME

I was thirteen and in no way could be called an athlete. But the one thing I had going for me was creativity. Thus was born Bobby Ball. Like me, the game is filled with endless losing. But most of all, naive hope.

Perhaps the greatest advantage of Bobby Ball is that unlike most sports, it doesn't require a whole lot of people to play. In fact, all it takes is two. And considering how few friends I had, this was a huge plus.

Sure, there were plenty of other games that only require one opponent, but I was most passionate about baseball. In fact, Bobby Ball was as close to competitive baseball as I got from middle school through high school.

Finding even one opponent certainly wasn't always easy. There were long stretches when I didn't have anyone. In the game's initial incarnation, my number one opponent was my three-year-old sister. I even batted left handed to give her a fair chance.

Not counting family members, I would say I had about five willing opponents during that span. There was a strong likelihood that most of them were far less interested in the game and far more interested in repeatedly walloping my ass to boost their own egos. As for me, I was just happy to have someone to play with.

So what exactly is Bobby Ball? On the surface, it is a cross between wiffle ball and dodgeball. It uses a wiffle ball bat along with a deflated rubber ball, halfway between the size of a baseball and a softball. It makes use of ghost runners and bean-outs. At its core, it's the baseball equivalent of one-on-one basketball. First one to twenty-one runs wins. Or, for a quick game, you can play until eleven.

From a cardiovascular perspective, Bobby Ball is a fantastic workout, consisting of virtually non-stop sprinting. I've never endured more soreness in any athletic endeavor than I have in the game that bears my name. My most athletic opponents over the years would agree. Even the ones in fantastic shape became winded.

Bobby Ball is not for the faint of heart. Getting beaned by a ball can make an impressive welt. Or, in the case of my friend Steve, legging out a single to first can lead to a ruptured Achilles heel. Bobby Ball beanings scarred me for life. Even when I'm playing softball, I duck and throw my arms over my head while running the bases out of fear of getting plunked in the noggin.

In the early days of the sport, it was played in the backyard of my childhood home, adjacent to my basketball court. However, after we broke a neighbor's window, it was time to seek greener pastures, which turned out to be in a small clearing in the woods across the street.

Home runs now had to clear a fence into someone's yard, forcing us to constantly trespass. "We," more often than not translated into "me," forced to retrieve my opponent's home runs. Before long, however, home runs were constantly clearing the house itself. We had outgrown that field just like the previous one and had to find a new home. We eventually relocated to the grounds of my elementary school, where I could battle my old grade school demons with every whiff of the bat.

Although I stopped keeping track of Bobby Ball statistics years ago, it would be generous to suggest that I have a lifetime .200 winning percentage. If anything, that number might more fairly represent my lifetime batting average, or, even more pathetically, my slugging percentage, though I could certainly knock one out of the park from time to time. It helped to imagine the faces of my bullies on the ball.

The layout of the elementary school field was just about perfect, emulating proportionate dimensions of a real baseball field, complete with a fence that ran at an angle from left to right, giving right-handed hitters a huge advantage. On the other side of the fence was not only home run territory, but a daycare center playground. If daycare recess was in session, we would have to either find a temporary location or postpone our game and find something else to do.

The infield was the blacktop used for elementary school kickball games, so sliding was out of the question. The grassy outfield featured a giant tree in center field, dubbed the Green Monster. Unless one cleared the tree, the branches would gobble up the ball. The ball remained in play until it landed on the ground, so we would have to wait beneath its limbs as the ball bounced around like a pinball, hoping that when the tree was through with it, we'd be in a good enough position to catch it. Sometimes, it never came down at all, at which point the batter was out and the game paused momentarily in order to first locate, and then retrieve the ball by throwing a shoe or the bat at it until it came back to earth. On occasion, the ball was either never located, or was too lodged between branches to get down, destined to spend eternity above the field, which meant heading to Toys "R" Us to find a new ball. It also meant the person responsible for hitting it into the tree automatically lost. Same if a home run landed on the roof of the school, or if a bat were to somehow defy physics and break in half. (This happened once, following years of abuse.)

Due to the quirky nature of Bobby Ball and the unique obstacles that come with each field, rules sometimes had to be made up on the fly. This led to the occasional argument and accusations of cheating. However, all I had to do was play the "the-game-is-named-after-me-and-I-make-up-all-the-rules" card to end any disagreement. Besides, it's a safe bet that most of my opponents didn't care about this game as much as I did. They were too busy playing real sports, and Bobby Ball was just a fun way to defeat me.

But once a new Bobby Ball rule was in the rulebook, it was pretty much set in stone, at least, until I decided to brandish my chisel to change a rule if I later deemed it necessary. Though I wasn't a winner at my own game, it was the one area of sports where I could exert authority

For example, a rule adopted early on was that any ball hit up in the air in the infield had to be caught in the air. However, anything in the outfield could be caught on one bounce for an out. Due to my inability to judge traditional fly balls, the one-bounce rule increased my fielding percentage exponentially.

Another quirk located in shallow left field was a funnel ball chute. If a ball landed in there, the batter would get as many runs as indicated by the hole that the ball eventually dropped out of. Nobody ever accomplished this feat. But it made the rulebook, nonetheless. Leave it to me to make a rule for something that literally never happened.

Despite the losing, it eventually gave me the confidence I needed to give baseball a chance. It was during my junior year when I finally mustered up the courage to try out for my school's JV team. Though I didn't make the cut, at least I tried. Despite this setback, I took comfort in the fact that there was always Bobby Ball. It was much more fun, anyway.

As the years went by, one thing has been constant—my losing record in all things sports. At least I was consistent, as a fan, player, and coach. And somehow, it was easier to lose at my namesake game, where I'd made up all the rules.

Though it has been years since I moved away from the fields of my youth, I continually seek out new fields of dreams. Even now, whenever I pass a clearing or a park, it is my instinct to naturally envision how the dimensions of a particular space would potentially lend itself to the game of Bobby Ball. It's a potential, personal field of dreams, where over time, the universe will balance things out so that I will someday have a winning record to call my own.

9

PRANK CALL

Suspect number one.

When you are a middle school misfit and the pickings are slim, there is a certain level of desperation that can lead to questionable friendship choices. Sometimes, you end up caught in the crossfire of behavior that you normally would not participate in, knowing full well the consequences that lay in store. Sometimes, you become a fall guy.

For a *very* brief period of time, my entire social circle consisted of two ne'er-do-well brothers from across the street who had recently moved in from out of state. Though I can't seem to recall where they moved from, I do seem to recall thick southern accents, which means they came from somewhere down south. Since I lived in Michigan, this could have very well meant Ohio.

I can't for the life of me remember their names. I think I've blocked it out. But one was my exact age, the other a year or two older. And they both had a distinct smell—not quite body odor, but like a crossbreed of dirty gym shoes and mold. I've never smelled anything like it since.

For many reasons, my parents weren't too thrilled with my new social circle. As much as my parents hoped I could make some friends, they at least maintained a certain level of standards. Nerds and dorks were fine. Burgeoning criminals, not so much.

As it turned out, their judgment proved accurate. These two were nothing but trouble.

For starters, the ne'er-do-wells rarely went to school. They were a modern day Ewell family. Secondly, they cussed up a storm. My parents were certainly not prudes, but these boys sure loved to cuss it up every chance they got, whether parents—their own or mine—were around or not. They also had a propensity for setting things on fire, blowing things up, throwing rocks and sticks at people or through windows, and participating in various forms of vandalism. In many ways, they were the precursor to Sid from *Toy Story*.

I was adept at staying out of situations that could either get me hurt or get me in trouble. Most of the time, I was the one tattling on other people. Yet somehow, I got wrapped up with the two stooges simply because they let me hang out with them and they were literally a stone's throw away.

One day, after riding our bikes up and down dirt piles located behind the school for several hours, we headed back to their house to hang out. Their house smelled just like them but *worse*.

Nobody was home, so naturally, they took me into their parents' bedroom to show me their dad's *Penthouse* collection. I had never seen porn of any kind before. They actually gave me a copy to sneak home. I knew I could get in trouble, but what middle school boy could resist?

We then headed into the living room, where they proceeded to put a porn video on and started to masturbate in separate corners of the room, as I stared at the TV, with a closed porno mag in my lap, giving serious thought as to whether I wanted to continue this relationship.

The brothers were befuddled as to why I wasn't participating. Apparently, I was the weird one.

When they were done, the eldest said, post-coitally, "Hey, let's make some prank calls! To the police station!" His brother couldn't jump aboard his bandwagon more quickly. After they zipped up their pants, they headed into the kitchen. I followed haplessly behind, thinking I should really head home.

In hindsight, that certainly would have been for the best.

In my middle school logic, I could quietly accept the brotherly masturbation session, but I had to speak up about prank calls.

"Guys, I don't know about this..." I said, ever the party pooper.

"Why not?" the older one asked.

"Why not?" I said, attempting to be the voice of reason. "We can get into a lot of trouble!"

"We do it all the time!" the younger one said.

"You do?"

"Don't worry. We don't dial 911. Just the front desk."

Maybe it was just me, but pranking the police in any shape or form seemed to be asking for trouble.

So once again, I found myself going along with something I had no desire to partake in. I convinced myself that as long as it wasn't happening on my parents' phone, I had nothing to worry about.

The eldest dialed.

"Dearborn Police," a voice said on the other end. "How may I help you?"

"Help! My mom is getting molested by a midget!"

"Excuse me?" an exasperated voice said on the other end of the phone.

"My mom! She needs help. A midget it assaulting her and trying to kidnap her. He's got knives. Please come save her!"

He then hung up and the brothers burst into hysterics.

Meanwhile, I couldn't help but wonder, did he make that story up on the spot? Or, did he plan it out ahead of time? I wasn't sure which was more likely, or more impressive. All I knew is, it was time to get the hell out of there. I had seen enough for one day.

It wasn't until I was safely in my own room that I realized what I was holding in my sweaty fingers. The porno mag! What was I thinking? Why did I take it home? I hid it deep in a desk drawer, beneath some Batman comics and Sea-Monkey manuals.

As my family gathered around the dinner table, eating barbequed chicken, my mom asked about my outing.

"It was okay," I said.

"What did you do?"

"Road our bikes. Played Nintendo. Nothing too exciting."

"I just wish you would find some other friends."

Yeah, me too.

And then I spotted something that made me nearly choke on my chicken. A cop car parked in the driveway across the street.

"Some friends you have there," my dad said.

I tried to play it cool. But playing it cool was something I was incapable of in any capacity. With each passing second, my anxiety increased.

"Why aren't you eating?" my mom asked.

I took a bite of Uncle Ben's rice pilaf. And that was when I noticed three of Dearborn's finest approaching the house. Complete with matching moustaches.

"Why are they coming here?" my dad asked. He got up to answer the door. And why three of them? Dramatic purposes, I suppose.

"Is there something wrong, officers?"

"We believe your son may have pranked called the station," one of the officers informed my father.

"Bobby! Get over here!"

I sheepishly approached the door.

"Did you prank the police?"

I shook my head.

The police officers and my dad stared at me sternly.

"Come on," another officer said. "Tell us the truth."

And then through a cascade of tears, I fessed up.

"You realize," said the cop with the thinnest 'stache, "young man, that this is a very serious offense?"

I nodded. I said nothing about the kids across the street. Not one word. I didn't tell the police it had been their idea. I didn't tell the police I hadn't dialed or spoke or anything except stood there, desperate to go home.

My dad was fuming.

"Can you promise us you won't do it again?" the officer with the thickest 'stache said.

I nodded through tears.

"Sorry about that officer," my dad said. "Bobby, apologize to these officers."

"I'm so sorry," I said, crying even harder.

"Have a good night," the officer with the medium 'stache said. They then turned around and headed down the sidewalk.

So why exactly did I take the fall? Easy. It came down to a simple formula: desperate for friends + scared of retaliation = desperate measures.

In other words, I was less afraid of getting in trouble with the law than I was of retribution from the kids across the street.

My parents were outraged. They took away all my TV and video game time. They also forbid me from playing with the stinky ne'er-do-wells ever again.

This meant I was right back where I started—in desperate need of friends. Only now, the police knew where I lived and I was also possibly a criminal.

Oh, well. At least I got to keep the porn magazine.

10

SUCKER SLAP

Bad Breath Bugle Boy in all his finery.

THERE COMES a point in life when a person realizes that

enough is enough. Deep in the misery of fifth grade, following years of taunts and ridicule, I reached that point.

Throughout elementary school, I endured an abundance of bullying. It varied in theme and tone, but never in intensity. Most of it was physical, but certainly not all of it. My bullies enjoyed messing with my head, too.

Some psychologists would say that emotional bullying is far worse than any form of physical, even if physical bullying included being tied to a tree, or having your face shoved in dogshit. I'm no psychologist, but I will tell you this: neither one is any fun.

The champion of my emotional bullying was a boy named Andy. Andy wasn't the most popular kid in class, and he wasn't that much bigger than me. Yet somehow, I became his main target. He was probably trying to gain a rung on the social ladder by constantly putting down someone just slightly beneath him in the pecking order.

Although Andy didn't physically harm me like so many others of his ilk, his taunts still stung. So much for the old adage that "sticks and stones may break your bones, but words will never hurt you." Words did hurt me. A lot.

Andy also had the unique ability to say things to me under his breath when nobody else was listening or within earshot. This way, he could slowly break me down, like verbal water torture. Drip by drip.

A sampling:

"Nobody likes you."

"Nobody is ever going to want to kiss you/love you/marry you."

"You have bad breath." He always liked to comment on my bad breath. Whether or not my breath was actually bad, I never really knew for sure. But I took his word for it.

All his words.

In response, I consumed quite a lot of gum, mints, and

breath spray, but the more mint he smelled on my breath, the more he seemed to tell me how badly my breath stunk. I was convinced there was no amount of mint in the world that could freshen my breath.

For some reason, the breath insults bothered me more than so many of the seemingly far worse things he told me. He single-handedly took my breath from me. And shattered my already pencil-thin social confidence.

Andy also had a propensity to remind me of the long list of embarrassing things I had done, or had been done to me over the years.

As though I would ever forget.

Sometimes, he preferred to mimic my speech impediments, even the ones that were long gone.

Though Andy never laid a hand on me, he loved to pretend to hit me, which in turn, made me flinch. This way, he never had to worry about getting in trouble for punching me, but he could get off on my consistent reaction, which was just shy of curling into a ball.

But then the day finally came for me to lay a hand on him.

Scene: elementary school cafeteria. I was sitting alone, despite being surrounded by peers at a packed table, chomping on my bologna sandwich. Oscar Meyer. On Wonder Bread. With a healthy spread of French's yellow mustard. Andy decided to squeeze in right across from me, where he proceeded to make fun of the way I was chewing. Now, I've always been a horrible chewer, and I knew it. Andy loved to remind me.

"Hey, Bugle Boy!" Andy said, still mimicking my chomps. "Wat'cha got there? Bologna? Aren't your worried about your breath?"

I ignored him, even though I was crying inside.

I couldn't even swallow the bite of bologna in my mouth. Combined with the white, mushy bread, it had turned into more of a paste in my mouth. With a hint of mustard.

"Maybe I should call you Bugle Breath! Hey, Bugle Breath!"

I was losing my grip. I could feel everything I was holding in beginning to work its way out.

"Oh oh! Looks like Bugle Breath is about to cry. What are you going to do about it?"

I ignored him, but then he threw a figurative gut punch. "Better ask your mommy to call Lifeline!"

Them were fighting words.

My mom was not only a lunch lady a hundred feet away, but she worked for the emergency call system, Lifeline, leading to constant taunts mimicking the famous 80s commercial with the little old lady proclaiming, "I've fallen and I can't get up!"

Looking back, something like that really shouldn't have been embarrassing. But my classmates simply turned it into something embarrassing by incessantly teasing me about it. Perhaps if I never let on that it bothered me, it would have stopped. But that was my problem. I always let on.

As Andy kept taunting me and my mother, I felt something unfamiliar boiling deep beneath the surface. Something I could no longer contain.

Rage.

Up until that point, I had always found turning the other cheek to be a convenient way to cope. But not now. Not this time. Passive resistance can only work for so long. It was time to take to the streets. You don't talk about a boy's mama without a fight.

Maybe all it would take was one solid punch to rid myself of this bullying curse once and for all, just like the movies lead me to believe. If it worked for *The Karate Kid*, it could work for me. And if I went down, at least I would go down swinging. Just look at *Rocky*.

But this was no movie.

One thing was clear, I had reached the point of no return and gave it my best shot. Unfortunately, all of my suppressed, accumulated rage could muster up was one half-assed, weak slap across my bully's cheek, filled with a bologna sandwich of his own.

Not a sucker a punch.

A sucker slap.

Andy's immediate reaction was to laugh, then choked on his bite (a brief, moral victory). When he recovered, he continued eating his sandwich as though nothing had happened. Meanwhile, the dozen or so witnesses also laughed, then got back to their far more popular existence.

I was beneath notice. Even a slap from me was beneath notice.

Adding insult to injury, this incident prompted even more teasing by my bully.

I remained Bad Breath Bugle Boy.

And my bullies now knew that even if I tried to do something about it, they didn't have to fear serious retribution.

But what may have been only a mild graze to Andy felt like a knockout punch to me. I had stood up. I had fought back. Me, Bobby Bugle Boy had actually taken a stand.

Maybe tomorrow, I wouldn't. Maybe tomorrow, I would cry. Maybe tomorrow, I would run to my mother. But today, I had hit Andy back. Today, I was Rocky and the Karate Kid all rolled into one fifth grader who wore a Sea-Monkey necklace and went by the name Bugle Boy.

That's Mr. Bugle Boy with minty-fresh breath to you.

11

AIR BALL

I may have been a dork, but I kept my teeth clean.

MIDDLE SCHOOL IS AWKWARD ENOUGH for anyone, but a nightmare for any perceived dork, nerd, or weirdo. Being the caboose on the puberty train certainly didn't help matters, either.

The bane of my middle school existence was gym class, just as it was in elementary school. But now, it was a daily nightmare instead of a semi-weekly one.

And wouldn't you know it, this was also the point when I *finally* became interested in sports. It was almost like my bullied mind figured that becoming interested in sports would somehow normalize me in the eyes of my peers.

The first major step in my sports development occurred during the summer before seventh grade, when my parents installed a basketball hoop on our backyard driveway. My whole family christened the court by carving our initials into the pole's concrete base, and I was sure that once the cement dried, I'd be on my way to NBA superstardom.

Never mind that our driveway wasn't really meant to be a basketball court. The "baseline" ran along the edge of the grass, but it was more of a curve than a line, making it a challenge to keep the ball inbounds. To compound matters, the court itself consisted of several large, uneven concrete slabs, featuring crooked raised ridges that were extremely tricky to navigate. If you dribbled just so, the ball would ricochet in a gazillion different directions, but more often than not, it ricocheted directly into your face or nuts.

If the ball landed on the lawn, it was quite likely to bounce into a pile of dogshit. If the ball were to land in dogshit, the hope was that it would land on an old, dusty, dry pile, rather than a steaming fresh one that would get smeared into the ball's small indentations like water into a sponge. If there was ever a great motivator to develop adept ball-handling skills, it was dogshit.

Even with a substandard court, I soon became obsessed

with basketball. Sun, rain or snow, my hoop was there for me. There was no "off-season." Not even the dead of winter could stop me. As long as I had a shovel, I was good to go, icicle fingers and all. When the climate got too extreme, there was always my bedroom Nerf hoop that my feeble mind decided to hang over a window, which I eventually shattered on a monster jam against myself.

I also hoped that having my own basketball court would help my social life. I had no shortage of enemies, but what would I do about opponents? The handful of friends I had weren't exactly into sports. When word slowly got out that I had a brand new hoop, however, it was a huge surprise as to how popular I suddenly became. We would play deep into the night, the court illuminated by garage light. Once, during a birthday sleepover, we headed outside to play at three in the morning. My parents received a knock on the door. Standing on the porch was a man in cut-off shorts who told my sleepy-eyed parents, "I'm the neighbor from behind. Please tell the kids to stop." So we waited until later that morning to resume our game.

I never shot a basketball more consistently than I did in my backyard, but only when shooting baskets by myself, accompanied by the musical stylings of C+C Music Factory, LL Cool J, MC Hammer, Vanilla Ice, and DJ Jazzy Jeff & the Fresh Prince.

To compensate for my deficiencies, I somehow managed to develop a bag of elaborate, body-twisting circus trick shots that I could perform expertly when playing by myself, but could never come close to replicating in actual game situations, much akin to the singing-in-the-shower effect. Somehow, my trick shots had a higher shooting percentage than traditional shots. Even so, I just didn't make that many baskets. And the ones I usually made were usually more of a matter of luck than of skill.

In the court of my imagination, however, I ruled supreme, firing off a never-ending parade of down-to-the-wire, game-winning dunks. In my mind, I was Isiah Thomas, Joe Dumars, and Bill Laimbeer. I grabbed rebounds exactly like Dennis "the worm" Rodman—or so I thought. In reality, I played basketball the way I did everything, off the grid of normalcy.

Despite my shortcomings, nothing could erode my newly formed obsession with the sport. When I wasn't playing basketball, I was watching it. I became a Pistons fan during the playoff run that resulted in the second of their back-to-back championships (1989-1990). I regretfully missed out on their first one, only to faithfully latch onto a team that quickly faded into ineptitude through the 90s, where there were more losing seasons than winning ones. Leave it to me to root for a team going downhill.

With my newly acquired "skills," the time had come to suit up for real, joining a recreational basketball league. My team was the Nuggets. We finished in last place. I once scored two points in a game. They were the only points I scored all season, but they were mine all the same.

Looking back on that team, I most remember Bronco, a beastly, but sweet-natured, dough-faced kid of some undetermined ethnicity who wore Coke-bottle glasses with thick frames. During games, whenever Bronco got the ball into his hands, his father incessantly screamed out in a nearly indecipherable accent, "Bronco! Shoot the ball! Bronco! Shoot the ball! Shoot the ball, Bronco!" And sure enough, whenever Bronco got the ball in his hands, he *always* shot it. Open or not, it didn't matter. The dude never passed. He was, after all, doing what his dad told him to. He never scored, and he lead the team in offensive fouls.

A year later, I left the hell of middle school and entered the jungle of high school. I decided to give recreational basketball another shot by joining a YMCA league. Halfway through the season, I somehow managed to score seven points in a game, which raised my season PPG average to 1.6. With each shot, I could feel something peculiar and unfamiliar growing inside me: hope. My culminating seventh point was a wide-open three pointer drained with a swish. It was the pinnacle of my basketball career. I felt invincible.

Buoyed by my long-awaited tenth grade growth spurt, my athletic confidence reached a point where I decided to try out for the JV basketball team. Deep down, I knew I had little chance of making it, but even deeper down, I believed anything is possible. Of course, reality dictated otherwise. It wasn't meant to be. Neither was it meant to be for my friend Patrick, who—despite being the tallest person to try out—failed to make the team as well. As upset as I was for both of us, his failure to make the team was a bittersweet consolation for me. Aside from having no skill, I was also short for my age. Patrick had both skill and size on his side.

I took solace in my backyard hoop, which was always there for me. It was my recreation, my boredom-buster, and sometimes, my therapy.

One cold, gray fall day, my parents found out I was failing an AP Government class I had no business taking. Depressed and frustrated, I headed outside and shot baskets until I started feeling better. Later, when I found my calling as a writer, my hoop served double duty as a distraction whenever I needed a break or to dribble plot complications out of my mind until my brain worked the problem out with a jump shot of creativity.

I think about that old hoop from time to time. I like to imagine that it still stands. I like to imagine that the cracks in the concrete are probably even more severe and dangerous for even the greatest of dribblers. Despite all of these flaws, I like to imagine that the court is still played on. I like to imagine that whoever plays on it now has a better winning percentage than I did. And even if the hoop is gone, I am hopeful that the concrete slab with my family's initials remains, serving as both a tribute and memorial that we once lived there. A ghost of our former existence, permanently fixed in time, and—like me—never giving up.

12

THE ART OF TZU

I was waiting on a snowy street corner for my ride when I spotted a peculiar Asian kid around my age, approaching me at a brisk clip. He seemed to walk on his tippy toes, his nose pointed in the air. He had passed me by several times before and I was curious.

In 1993, when an Asian family suddenly appeared in my hometown, people took notice. It wasn't that I had no exposure to diversity. I grew up in Dearborn, Michigan, home of the largest Arab community outside of the Middle East. Asians, however, weren't even a blip on the demographic radar.

I had never seen him prior to this school year and figured since he was probably new to the 'hood, he could use a friend. I knew I did. And it was nice to know that there was possibly someone who felt as out of place as I did, even if it was for different reasons.

He passed by several times for weeks, without acknowledging me. My attempts to make eye contact with him were futile. He was in a world of his own.

I finally decided to break the ice—or rather, the snow—by

picking up a compacted chunk of snow the plows had left behind. I held it out to him as he drew near.

"What do you think of this?" I asked. If it was strange for a fifteen-year-old to come up to a stranger and make a non-sequitur, he didn't comment on it.

Instead, he said, "It's huuuge," with a thick accent. "Where'd you find it?"

His response was almost as bizarre as my question. That was the extent of my first conversation with Tzu (pronounced "zoo"), but I knew we'd be friends.

However, following our initial encounter, he didn't pass by the next day. Or, the day after that. I logically assumed I scared him off and that he'd decided to take a different route. I certainly couldn't blame him. If a weirdo offered you a giant chunk of ice out of the blue, most people would be apt to seek a different path.

Not me. I would have assumed I'd found my doppelganger.

It would be over a week before I saw him again. But this time, it wasn't on the corner. It was from my own backyard where I was shooting hoops. I looked across five or six yards and there he was. Shooting hoops in his own backyard. I figured I had nothing to lose, so I headed down the street and officially introduced myself. He introduced himself as Dave (his American name), before starting an impromptu game of one-on-one. He beat me. In years to come, he would always beat me.

After our game, I discovered that Tzu, who was two years older than me, had moved from Taiwan to Michigan a couple of years before. He attended my high school, but I had never once seen him there, which was a surprise, considering he was one of the only two Asians in the building, the other being his sister, Wei. I never saw her, either.

"So why do you go by Dave?" I asked when I discovered his real name was Tzu.

"Because the principal thought it would be easier for everyone to pronounce if I had an American name."

For the same reason, Wei was re-branded "Wendy." Yes, they were named after the fast food Dave and Wendy.

I never called him Dave again.

We played ball the next day, this time at my house. After Tzu dunked a game-winning lay-up, his foot landed on a fresh pile of dogshit.

"Oh no! I stepped in dog's poo!" he said in his thick accent. He became extremely distressed over this incident, far more than warranted. I got the sense that he had never stepped in dogshit before and perhaps didn't know how to properly handle it. I located a twig for him to dig out the smeared, caked shit from the bottom of his shoe. I then grabbed the pooper-scooper to retrieve the smashed pile off of the ground. I sprayed the remnants off his shoe and concrete with a hose. I consider this the exact moment that our friendship firmly took root.

Furthermore, something about this incident must have awakened the beast inside him because he shut me out 21-0 in the next game. As I quickly learned, it wasn't a fluke. His court or mine, it didn't make a difference. The results were the same and the only real difference was that his rim was much lower, which meant constantly getting dunked on by a short Asian. I don't believe I ever once dunked on him.

Although we routinely played ball in his yard, it would be almost a year before I was actually invited into his house. And I was rarely allowed in after that. I found it odd, but it wasn't any of my business, though I was certainly intrigued. I couldn't help but envision an Asian Boo Radley lurking behind the curtains. But then I finally got to see for myself.

Despite my preconceived notions, there was nothing unusual about the inside of his house once you got past the Asian spices wafting in the air. Tzu showed me the "rice closet," an entire closet stacked with enormous bags of white rice. We all have neighbors we can rely on to borrow a cup of sugar. Tzu's house was the place to go if the need arose to borrow a cup—or a gallon—of rice. It also explained the constant source of what Tzu referred to as his "rice farts."

Once, I brought my old Tyco slot-car track over—a toy that had been collecting dust downstairs on a shelf—and set it up in Tzu's basement. When I asked for it back a few weeks later, he told me that his father had thrown it out.

"Why?" I asked.

"Because he didn't want it," Tzu explained matter-of-factly.

"So he threw it away?"

Tzu shrugged it off, but I was never allowed in the house again and left with the empty void of knowing that one of my favorite childhood toys was now gone forever. Though I couldn't be certain, my theory was that his father was so against his children acclimating themselves to American culture that he was willing to do whatever he could to repel potential American friends away from him. Made more sense than just about anything else I could drum up in my mind. But I still wanted my racetrack back.

Eventually, I worked up the courage to ask Tzu why I was not welcome in his house.

"You're not Asian," he said confirming my theory, before he added, "Just kidding!"

He wasn't.

From what I was able to cobble together, Tzu lived with his father and sister. His mother had remained in Taiwan for reasons Tzu never really made clear to me. He insisted that his parents weren't separated, despite keeping half a world between them. He gave me the impression that his mother's return home was imminent, but that day was still years away. He later confessed that his mother didn't like it in America, so she simply went back home.

Tzu filled a niche that my other friends didn't and made me

realize there were other options out there. Tzu wasn't a band geek like all my other friends. He shared my passion for sports, providing a gateway into a world that had previously rejected me. Suddenly, I felt insulated against my enemies. Whenever we hung out, it usually involved sports, whether it was playing them, watching them, or playing sports-themed video games in between episodes of *Beavis & Butthead*. According to Tzu, he was destined for greatness in Taiwan as a pitcher, until he severely hurt his knee. Also, according to Tzu, he was a distant relative of tennis legend Michael Chang.

I'd finally found my way into the wide world of sports and Tzu was my mentor. He taught me about sports from the inside out, especially baseball and basketball. I didn't exactly get better at sports, though he did sort of teach me how to pitch, but I *understood* them more. And grew more passionate as a result. He also made it feel safe to play sports, unlike the tormentors from my past who teased me for my athletic ineptitude.

Brimming with false confidence, I finally found the courage to try out. In basketball, Tzu made me think that I actually had a shot (though it was my *lack* of a shot that ultimately prevented me from making the team). It was my general lack of hand-eye coordination, strength, and sufficient bat speed that led to me not making the baseball squad. Never made it past the first round of cuts in either sport.

Despite my ever-expanding losing record against him in all thing sports, including video games, Tzu gave me the confidence to keep playing no matter how badly I sucked. Playing ball with Tzu made me feel like I was now part of the club. And even though I consistently lost, I was having fun doing it.

And that was everything.

I just wish I had friends who were worse at sports than me so I could actually stand a chance in hell of actually winning.

Every now and then, lightning would strike and I would actually eke out a victory, although I always suspected that Tzu let me win. There were also countless games that I should have won, or almost won, but didn't. I would either have a big lead that I choked away, or I would fold under the pressure of a close game, suddenly unable to hit a single shot to save my life.

I think I never really learned how to win.

Over the years, I have made little progress in that regard. As Tzu helped me realize time and time again, winning is something that someone is either born with or—in my case—*isn't.*

In addition to being the anchor to the wide world of sports, Tzu quickly became a fixture in my family, almost like a surrogate adopted Asian brother. He came over just about every day, especially that first summer of our friendship.

If my mom finished making dinner while he was over, he joined us at the table. Large extended family gatherings? He was there. He was *absorbed* into us. An honorary member of our family. Even though his father continued to shut me out of his world, Tzu was growing more and more "Americanized," which I always suspected was his father's greatest fear. The lack of an Asian population to preserve his culture with made it even easier for him to disappear into the fabric of the new world.

Aside from becoming a fixture in my family's life, Tzu became a free math tutor for not just me, but my siblings too, thus fulfilling the stereotype. In fact, Tzu not only tutored me, but he also bailed me out of my failing geometry class, using his position as the teacher's assistant. I didn't understand one bit of the subject matter, and it didn't help that the teacher was an old curmudgeon who may have been an ancestor of Ebenezer Scrooge.

One day, while inputting grades, Tzu noticed that I was about to receive an E for the quarter and then managed to convince the old coot to bump it up to a D minus. It was the worst grade I ever got in my life, but I passed. Who knows what would have become of my life if I failed? I'd probably be in the same place I am now—living a math-free existence.

Not everyone thought of Tzu as my brother, though. One summer, he brought an Asian friend along to a family barbeque, prompting my southern-bred grandmother to shout out from across the room, "Those Chinese boys are eating all the chicken wings!"

It was at this same event that Tzu got completely trashed. Half passed out on the couch, my dad asked him, "Hey, Tzu? How many drinks did you have?"

"Don't know," he said. "Double digits."

Till this day, my family still refers to excessive drinking as "double digits."

Tzu could be very blunt at times. His stock reply to a question he didn't feel like answering was, "Why you care?" It didn't matter if the question was personal or impersonal. It was how he answered *most* questions.

It's important to note that Tzu had a knack for getting overly cocky when it came to sports. Some might call it overly competitive. Once, he was hot-dogging a bit too much for my uncle's liking and was called out for it. As my Uncle asked for Tzu to throw him the ball back, Tzu snapped back at him, "Go suck on your own balls."

In front of my entire extended family.

He then stormed off the field, in pursuit of more double digits.

Shortly after that, we began to drift apart. He graduated two years before me, and during my senior year of high school, he announced that he was joining the Air Force in order to help pay for college.

I was crushed.

He was stationed in Dayton, Ohio, so he came home often.

But he might as well have been a different person. Anytime any of us would ask him how he was doing, he would respond, "Top secret. Classified." We couldn't possibly take this seriously. Yet, he expected us to go along with it.

There was no question that the military changed him. He also developed a keen interest in partying, while I still preferred to stay home on a Saturday to laugh my ass off at *Mystery Science Theater 3000*.

After four years, Tzu's military service ended and he returned home. We started hanging out again on a regular basis, but he was still more interested in going to bars and getting drunk with his cooler buddies than he was hanging out with me. Suddenly, Tzu was an older version of the bullies who used to torment me in grade school. The funny little Asian that I had grown to love had become an all-American asshole.

Though our friendship was still always there, just beneath the surface, it no longer took center stage like it had for that two-year period that began with a block of ice on a suburban street corner. But I still valued his friendship, and when it came time for my wedding, I asked him to be my best man.

In the months leading up to marriage, I decided to give weightlifting another try for the first time in ten years, prompted by my Ukrainian fiancée and her family who complained that I was too skinny to be worthy of their daughter. Tzu volunteered to be my personal trainer and spotter, continuing our tradition of sports mentoring. Buoyed by Tzu's intense, *Karate Kid*-style training, I got into the best shape of my life. My bodybuilding regimen was also aided by whey protein shakes, which gave me the worst, most foul-smelling gas of my life. Worse than rice farts, even.

A few months later, my bachelor party finally arrived. I should have seen the writing on the wall when my request to do something low-key was met with resistance. I made it clear to Tzu that I was perfectly content with dinner and a Tigers game. *Maybe* followed by some mild bar hopping. Tzu, however, had a whole other idea. And it involved boobies. Though I wasn't surprised, I thought he would at least respect my wishes: No strip clubs. No strippers.

He did not.

Before we headed to Detroit, a small group of friends and family—a dozen or so in total—gathered at my parents' house for a quick beer. Tzu had informed us earlier that he would be meeting us downtown for unspecified reasons. I found this strange, but then again, wasn't entirely surprised.

When we got downtown, we ate at a crowded pub outside Comerica Park called The Elwood Bar & Grill. As we sat outside on the noisy open-air patio, the smell of hot dogs and stale beer wafted in from the stadium. Halfway through our meal, there was still no sign of Tzu.

Just as we were finishing up, he finally arrived, along with an entire uninvited posse. He stood in the middle of a scattered smorgasbord of former—and even current—bullies. They were the kind of jocks that say things like "bros before hos" and started bar fights to prove their manliness. These were Tzu's kind of people, not mine.

The initial group Tzu arrived with was maybe five or six deep. But more continued to arrive one by one, and before long, the uninvited party more than doubled my invited guests.

Tzu's band of merry douches were either oblivious to the fact that they were crashing a bachelor party they weren't invited to, or didn't give a shit. It was hard to tell which. I guess it depended on how Tzu had spun it to them. He certainly didn't go out of his way to introduce me to any of them. Due to limited seating capacity, his gang had to sit several tables away. Tzu didn't even make an effort to float between sections. He stayed with his party only, which added insult to injury.

It grew increasingly and abundantly clear that nobody there had come to my party. They had come to start their own. And

Tzu had clearly picked his cooler friends over me. Once again, I was being picked last in gym class, only this time, the person doing the picking was my best man.

"You know what this party needs?" one of Tzu's bros screamed out to a waitress. "More beer! Three pitchers, Coors, pronto!" As if ordering Coors was something exciting to do.

The annoyed waitress nodded.

I tried to focus on the friends who *didn't* let me down that night, but everyone knew what was going on and the awkwardness hung over our table like the smell of a rice fart. Conversation was stilted. Nobody laughed.

With the pitchers of shitty beer not even half gone, one of Tzu's buddies blurted out, "Man, this is just a bunch of dudes staring at one another. I thought we were gonna see some tits."

I couldn't quite make out what Tzu said in response, but next thing I knew, he was finally heading my way.

"Sorry, man. These guys are my ride. I gotta go."

He didn't even make a half-hearted effort to convince me to join them. He never asked.

Then he hugged me. Like Judas himself.

Just like that, my best man was gone.

And then the waitress brought their bill to my dad.

He was furious.

"You gotta be fucking shitting me."

Here was my dad's unofficially adopted son, betraying us. He threw his credit card on the table, his face turning red with anger, like a furnace about to explode.

As for me, I wanted to be furious, but could only feel the rejection and betrayal. An all-too-familiar gut punch.

I was an adult, about to be married, and yet I found myself drifting back to my elementary school playground. I suddenly didn't feel so grown up anymore. I'd almost forgotten how much it truly hurt. That deep, soul-searing rejection. Everything I thought I'd scarred over was ripped open again.

I can't say that Tzu completely ruined my night. Somehow, I compartmentalized his rejection to focus on the friends and family who had my back. And the relief of having all those dude-bros gone lightened up the party a lot. But afterwards, when I was alone, the pain came flooding in.

I barely slept that night. As I lay awake, I wondered what Tzu was feeling. Regret? Did he not even care at all? Or was he oblivious to everything? Which one was worse? And what next?

I finally drifted off to sleep.

When I woke up, I felt the familiar twinge of forgiveness rising form the beneath the pain. This came as no surprise. I have always been too quick to forgive. It's my defense mechanism against those who hurt me. Some might call it weak. I saw it as a way to release the pain and poison of transgression, resulting in a thicker skin made of scar tissue. Besides, I had to find a way to justify Tzu's actions in my own mind. How could I let him stand up for me as my best man if I didn't?

My dad saw things differently. Later that morning, Tzu showed up at my parents' house to apologize. My dad wasn't having it. He stormed into the living room in a fit of rage.

"You have real *balls*, Tzu! Real balls!"

I stood and watched helplessly as my mom tried to keep the peace, but my dad ignored her and continued to rip Tzu a new asshole. Tzu, to his credit, stayed mute. He had way too much respect for my dad to do anything other than take it, then leave with his tail between his legs

Our adopted family member had flown the coop.

I had no choice but to kick him out of my wedding party, a decision I have regretted ever since. Even after my first marriage ended, it didn't do anything to lessen my remorse. Booting him out of my wedding party was one thing, but informing him over e-mail was downright cowardly.

As it turned out, he didn't even show up to the ceremony.

The next time I saw him was several months later at another wedding, this one for a mutual friend. We didn't say a word to one another. In fact, it would be over a year before we did, at the same friend's bonfire. We awkwardly hugged, choosing to leave many things unsaid. We knew that we both felt the same way and hid behind our mutual shame.

At least the cold war was over.

After getting caught up with one another's lives, the main focus of our conversation naturally turned to sports: Tigers, Pistons, Lions. It was old times again. But yet, it wasn't. There was an unspoken truth between us that things could never really be the same again, as much as we would have liked. Even now, a decade after the incident, the scar beneath our friendship remains tender. Our mutual regret continues to burn beneath the surface. I suspect it always will.

We've hardly seen each other since that night. The next time I saw him was a couple of years later, when I attended Tzu's bachelor party. Guess where? I also attended his subsequent wedding, with the ghost of *my* wedding still hanging over our heads.

Incidentally, he married one of my friends, thereby completing his 180-degree American revolution.

In the years that followed, our paths periodically crossed. And each time, it was as though time somehow stood still. We talked about our favorite teams like before. We retreated into the safe world of sports. We still had that in common. We will always have that in common.

Since then, I've gotten both divorced and re-married. My second wife has met Tzu only once, at a friend's wedding. She was pregnant with our first child. I now have two kids and neither have ever met the closest thing I ever had to a brother growing up. I have only met one of Tzu's two kids, when his oldest was a newborn. That child is now approaching middle school.

Four years ago, I ran into him again at our friend's bonfire, the site of our truce nearly ten years before. It was a balmy, 72-degree October evening in Michigan—a rarity. A television was hooked up outside for game one of the MLB divisional series, Tigers against the A's. Tzu and I settled in to watch the game, side by side like we used to. Cheering our team on, but now only older, and possibly wiser.

I haven't seen him since.

13

WALK-OFF

Even as an adult, I never lost my love for sports. I had to give it one more try, and what was easier than softball? Not just softball, but co-ed softball. At my church. Surely I had found the teammates I was always meant to have.

I bought a brand-new glove, my first pair of cleats, my first cup, and my first non-wood bat—which turned out to be an absolute lemon. Yes, I was such a failure at sports, I was even a loser at *selecting* a bat.

Somehow, against all odds, I eventually turned out to be a fairly consistent hitter. I could at least get on base with a steady stream of singles.

Defense, on the other hand, was a whole other matter. For starters, I have always been afraid of the ball. I couldn't field a grounder if my life depended on it. And I completely lack the ability to judge fly balls. When a ball is hit my way, I either overrun it or stop short of it, watching it drop right in front of me, or more often than not, far away from me.

It should come as no surprise that the majority of my softball-related injuries have involved balls hit in the air—a testament to my lack of both geometry and physics skills.

For instance, one time I caught a pop up with my nose. Fortunately, despite the vast amount of blood, my nose wasn't broken, but my confidence certainly was. I would later require nasal septum surgery. This did nothing to alleviate my fear of the damn ball.

I'm still afraid.

And I still can't judge balls in the air very well.

My fear of the ball hinders my speed in other ways, too. For example, while running to first, I almost always duck and throw my arms over my head as I approach the base, thus slowing down and thereby resulting in outs that should have been hits. I firmly believe that softball leagues should require batters to wear helmets. I've considered wearing one to alleviate this phobia, but then I would look like an idiot. Or, more accurately, *more* of an idiot.

As far as my softball team itself, it was doomed from the start. Each week, I scrambled to find enough players. I guided my team to three straight, pitiful losing seasons before waving the white flag and putting it—and myself—out of our collective misery.

And yet, I just couldn't give up.

Following years of losing in all its various forms, one true moment of athletic glory finally arrived.

A year after my divorce, I was in a new, healthy and far more fulfilling relationship with—no kidding—a former state champion of track and field. The relationship was made all the better with the unexpected discovery that I was going to be a father. My daughter was due in late August, coinciding with the end of what had turned out to be a fantastic, turn-around season for my work's recreational softball team.

We ended the season tied for first, which meant having to play a one-game play-off for the championship on a chilly, rain-soaked late summer night. The game was a doozy, going back and forth all game long. Of course, I was conditioned to accept that a loss was always lurking around the corner. I was especially thinking this as I headed to the plate with the bases loaded in our final at-bat, down by one with two outs. After years of folding under pressure, there was no greater choke opportunity than that very moment. The fate of our entire season was now entirely up to me. And if past history was any indication, I was setting my team up to lose, and lose big.

Moments certainly don't get more pressurized than that. To compound matters, I wasn't having my best game at the plate to begin with, and I wasn't expecting it to change now.

But as I stood at the plate, I felt something shift within me. Perhaps it was seeing a glimpse of the new life that awaited me as a father. Perhaps I had simply willed myself to refuse to lose anymore. Perhaps it was all the feel-good sports movies I'd watched over the years. Whatever it was, I suddenly had the clarity I'd heard about, but never before experienced in sports.

The fear was gone.

And I knew exactly what I had to do.

Nothing was going to stop me.

I stepped into the pitch and swung, sending the ball sailing to right-center. The fielders who had come up shallow now had to sprint toward the backfield. The ball continued sailing through the night sky before arcing down and slamming down at the base of the fence. I had never come close to hitting a ball like this. I should point out that in this particular league, balls hit over the fence constitute outs. It would have been my luck to knock one out of the park and lose. But fate was on my side for once. And just like that, it was game over. We were champions.

Once upon a time, I was picked last in gym class.

And now, I was a champion.

If only my bullies could have seen me now. Then again, at that point, I could give two shits what they thought.

That was the real victory.

And even if my big hit didn't really mean anything in the grand scheme of things, I will never forget the feeling on that cold, wet summer night. In that singular moment, it meant everything.

That same night, just hours after our thrilling victory, came another one. I became a father. And I've been winning ever since. Professionally, the game-winning hit, combined with the birth of my daughter, mirrored my arrival as a published writer.

"Daddy doesn't give up," was one of my daughter's first phrases.

Though I had my share of losing in sports, I never took those losses too personally. Sure, they hurt, but I knew sports weren't my true destiny.

However, if there is anything I have lost at more consistently than sports, it's my writing. As any writer knows, there are always more rejections than acceptances. One can take only so many semi-finalist awards to begin feeling like you were destined to always be riding the bench.

But I never allowed a single rejection to rattle me. In fact, they only motivated me. They were my fuel. Every rejection was both a loss and a victory. Though a loss on the surface, each rejection is proof that I have not given up, that I have not lost my passion, my desire, my lifeblood after years of putting everything I have into a dream that has eluded me for so long. Somehow, that championship-winning hit was the catalyst for a consistent stream of publishing, which ultimately lead to the publication of my first book. And now this one.

Even though I still have an overall losing record—and probably always will—the fact that I continue playing makes me a champion, even if it's in a league all to myself.

I wouldn't have it any other way.

ACKNOWLEDGMENTS

I would like to thank each and every one of my bullies for making this book possible. Truly, thank you for pushing me onto the path that I never want to get off. It has been my yellow brick road.

Thank you to my editor Alex Kourvo, who wields the biggest knife in town. And in that knife, I put my full trust.

Thank you to the Ann Arbor District Library and Fifth Avenue Press, especially Erin Helmrich.

Thank you to Cultivate Coffee & Tap House. Sometimes a writer needs both caffeine and alcohol. You guys have it all figured out.

Special thanks to my parents, siblings, my Godmother Jo-Jo, Jon and Laurie Wilson, Jim Otto, Patti Smith, Vincent Daniels, Coach Samaha, Michael Ferro, Robin Gaines, Melissa Grunow, Frank Morelli, Randy Pearson, Dawn Richberg, Aimee Mepham, Jeff Gaynor, Sierra Elizabeth Hansen, Barbara Cataldo & Elaine Fleezanis (the two elementary school teachers that always made me feel safe), The Netural Zone, the Ann Arbor Area Writers Group (where I initially workshopped these essays), Patrick Benton, and Tzu Chang. And to all of my band friends, hang tight. I have an entire book in store for you. Just you wait.

And of course, the one person most responsible for my dream: my 10th grade English teacher Anne Gautreau, who helped me find my true self when I needed it most.

A special shout out to Dan Wolocko, who was the nicest kid in the whole school and the one popular jock who was nice to me. Seeing him at a recent class reunion only further reminded me of this fact.

Above all, thank you to Ellen, Lillian, and Bobby. Especially for your support during that one week in August. Living with a writer has to be the biggest pain in the butt, and yet, you somehow continue to tolerate it. The first piece in this collection was written shortly after my daughter was born six years ago. She's been my good luck charm ever since. Daddy loves you and your brother so much.

May this book remind every misfit out there that the only way to truly lose is to give up. Things will get better. Never stop swinging.

ABOUT THE AUTHOR

R.J. Fox grew up in Dearborn, Michigan. He's an independent filmmaker, saxophonist, and English teacher. His short stories, essays, and poetry have been published in over thirty literary magazines. He is the author of *Love & Vodka: My Surreal Adventures in Ukraine* and the forthcoming *Awaiting Identification.* R.J. teaches in the Ann Arbor Public Schools, where he uses his own experiences to inspire his students to follow their dreams.